SOME NOTA

THE VICTORIA CROSS **V.C.**	THE GEORGE CROSS **G.C.**	DISTINGUISHED SERVICE ORDER **D.S.O.**	THE MILITARY CROSS **M.C.**

THE GEORGE MEDAL **G.M.**	DISTINGUISHED CONDUCT MEDAL **D.C.M.**	MILITARY MEDAL **M.M.**	ROYAL RED CROSS **R.R.C.**

Series 606B

This carefully planned reference book will help to answer many of the questions that children ask.

Interesting and accurate information about the Army is given within the limits of a relatively simple vocabulary. Even children whose reading experience is limited will be encouraged to find out for themselves by the excellent full-colour illustrations and clear text, thus gaining extra reading practice.

A Ladybird 'Easy-Reading' Book

'People at Work'

The
SOLDIER

by I. & J. HAVENHAND
with illustrations by JOHN BERRY

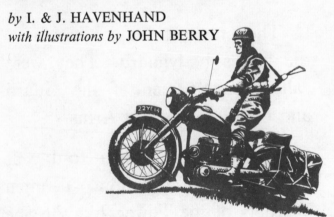

Ladybird Books Ltd Loughborough

THE SOLDIER

Just over three hundred years ago there were no full-time soldiers in this country to make up an army. Men became soldiers when the king needed them to fight a war. When the war ended the men went back to their homes.

The only regular soldiers were the king's bodyguard. They were called the Yeomen of the Guard and the Gentlemen at Arms.

You can see Yeomen to-day at the Tower of London. Yeomen Warders of the Tower, like the one in the picture, guard the tower where the Crown Jewels are kept.

7214 0070 1

After 1660, King Charles II kept a small army. The soldiers in this army were called Guards. Some of our soldiers to-day are still called Guards.

The soldiers of many years ago were either cavalrymen or infantrymen. The weapons of the infantrymen were pikes and muskets. Infantrymen fought on foot and were the tallest men in the army. They carried pikes which were sticks eighteen feet long with sharp metal points. The pikes were used against the enemy cavalrymen.

Later the infantrymen used muskets. These were big, clumsy guns from which metal balls were fired.

Pikes were not much used after the bayonet was invented by a Frenchman. A bayonet was a short sword which was fitted to the barrel of the musket.

The cavalrymen of the army rode into battle on horses. They fought with swords and pistols. The cavalrymen fired their pistols and then used their swords as they charged the enemy soldiers.

The soldiers all wore very brightly coloured uniforms. Each regiment had its own coloured jacket. Many of the uniforms had red jackets. People thought that soldiers in red would frighten the enemy.

As the years passed, more regiments were formed to make the army bigger. Better weapons were given to the soldiers and the colour of their uniforms was changed to the khaki colour that soldiers now wear.

When a man wants to be a soldier to-day, he goes to an office called the Army Information Office. There he has a talk with a man who is already a soldier.

After this he goes to a doctor who examines him. If the man is fit he can then become a soldier.

The new soldier goes to an army barracks where he meets other men who have just joined the army. At the barracks they are given their uniforms and begin to learn what they must do now that they are soldiers.

When men join the army they can choose what kind of soldiers they want to be. Some of them become infantrymen.

The uniforms and weapons of the infantrymen have changed from the olden days, but infantrymen are still the main fighting soldiers in the army.

Infantrymen do a lot of training to make themselves fit. They learn how to climb steep cliffs and how to use canoes. Sometimes they wear white clothes and learn how to ski so that they can fight in countries where there is thick snow.

Whatever kind of country they are fighting in, the infantrymen try to make it difficult for the enemy to see them. They wear nets over their helmets with twigs and leaves in them. At night they blacken their hands and faces so that these do not show.

Wherever there is fighting to be done the infantrymen are always there. They may have rifles or machine guns or even bigger guns that will stop tanks.

To-day, infantrymen are not just foot soldiers. Sometimes they walk, but often they ride in armoured fighting vehicles. These vehicles have tracks like tanks to help them cross rough ground.

At times helicopters carry infantrymen into battle. As the helicopters land, the soldiers leap out ready for action.

In battles to-day, tanks and armoured scout cars are used to help the infantrymen. The soldiers who use the tanks belong to the Royal Armoured Corps.

When horses were no longer needed, some of the cavalry regiments became armoured car regiments.

In an armoured car there is the driver and another soldier. This soldier acts as look-out, and sends radio messages to infantrymen or to soldiers in tanks. He also has a machine gun which he can fire through a slit in the turret of the armoured car and one which can be fired at aircraft.

Tanks of to-day are like moving forts, and move on tracks over rough country where other vehicles cannot go. Tanks are made of thick steel and carry big guns. These guns can fire shells a long way. Tanks also carry machine guns.

A tank commander rides with his head out of the turret. When there is danger, he closes the lid of the turret and joins the crew inside the tank.

The driver looks through a thick glass window when the tank goes into battle.

Big guns are used to help the infantry and tanks. These guns belong to the Royal Artillery, and fire shells at the enemy who may be a very long way off.

Some of the guns are towed to where they are needed, and spotters tell the gunners where to aim. A spotter may be a man on a hill top watching the enemy. Other spotters may be in small aeroplanes or helicopters.

The spotters radio to the gunners to tell them when they hit or miss the target.

Other guns of the Royal Artillery move on tracks like the tracks of tanks. These guns are called self-propelled guns.

Some regiments have guided weapons as well as guns. The men in these regiments fire large rockets which travel seventy miles or more. Smaller rockets or missiles are fired by gunners to destroy enemy rockets or planes.

The rockets may be guided to their target by radio messages or they may be set on target before firing. This means that they are made so that they find the target themselves.

Soldiers in the Royal Engineers have a special name and are called sappers. Wherever the tanks and infantry go, sappers are there to help them.

Sappers use special instruments to find, and make safe, mines that have been buried by the enemy. Mines are kinds of bombs that blow up when men walk on them, or when tanks and lorries go over them.

When roads and railways have been blown up, sappers mend them. They use bulldozers, cranes and other machines so that repairs can be done quickly and the army can move on.

If bridges have been blown up, sappers build new ones. Sometimes they use tanks with folding bridges on the top to make a way across small rivers.

Sappers can build a bridge in a night. If a river is very wide, the sappers build a bridge that floats on small boats called pontoons. Sappers make large rafts to ferry tanks and men across any rivers that are too wide for bridges.

In wartime, docks, railways, electricity works and water works can all be looked after by sappers of the Royal Engineers.

There are other kinds of engineers in the army and they belong to the Royal Electrical and Mechanical Engineers. These soldiers are skilled men who mend and look after all the special machines of the army.

After a battle, soldiers of the Royal Electrical and Mechanical Engineers collect tanks that have broken down or been damaged. These tanks are mended so that they can be used again.

Radios, watches, telephones, rockets, tanks and helicopters are among the many things that the soldiers mend in their work-shops.

In each regiment, soldiers do their own special kind of work. They may be in different places and many miles from each other. All the soldiers and regiments must work together as a large team.

The soldiers who belong to the Royal Corps of Signals make sure that messages and orders can always be delivered to the regiments in the army, wherever they are.

Some of the messages are carried by soldiers who ride motor-cycles. These soldiers are called despatch riders.

Other men in the Royal Corps of Signals run a telephone service. They lay the telephone wires and operate telephone exchanges.

Some regiments are always moving from place to place. Radios which can both pick up and send messages are used to keep in touch with these regiments. The soldiers who use the radios talk into microphones and listen through head phones.

All regiments of the army have radios in case the telephone wires get broken.

Secret messages and orders are sent in code.

Most of the soldiers in the Parachute Regiment are men from other regiments in the army who have asked to join it.

The soldiers who join must be very fit. They are trained to use all the infantry weapons and to be able to live and fight alone.

Before the soldiers make their first parachute jump they learn how to handle a parachute. They do this by hanging and swinging in parachute harness inside large hangars or from special towers.

The soldiers also learn how to land from a parachute drop so that they do not hurt themselves.

When the parachute soldiers have done their ground training they make their first jump. This is made from a large balloon which is fixed by a rope and is about eight hundred feet above the ground.

After the soldiers have made a second balloon jump they must do six more jumps from an aeroplane. One of these jumps is made at night.

The soldiers are then allowed to wear red hats, with badges that look like wings, to show that they belong to the Parachute Regiment.

Parachute soldiers are always ready to go anywhere in the world.

The soldiers of the Royal Army Ordnance Corps are the men who supply all the other soldiers in the army with everything they need.

They see that the soldiers have food, clothes, ammunition, petrol, tyres and even sweets and chocolate.

As the army moves forward, ammunition and other stores are carried in vehicles driven by men of the Royal Corps of Transport.

They carry tanks on very big lorries called tank transporters. They operate the military ports and railways and have special boats to carry men and tanks. Forward positions are supplied by Air Despatch Units dropping stores from aeroplanes.

Some men join the army and become cooks. They join the Army Catering Corps and are trained in big army kitchens. They also learn how to set up and use field kitchens. These kitchens are used when the army is in battle. When the cooks have been trained, they may go to any regiment they choose.

Other soldiers want to become bandsmen and they join one of the regimental bands. Some of these bandsmen are chosen for special training at the Military School of Music.

Sometimes soldiers become ill or they get hurt and have to see a doctor. The army has its own doctors and they belong to the Royal Army Medical Corps.

Every morning any soldiers who feel ill can ask to see a doctor. Army doctors examine the soldiers and give them medicine.

Some doctors are trained to drop with parachute troops so that they can be near if the soldiers need them. The doctors quickly help the wounded soldiers and send them to hospitals.

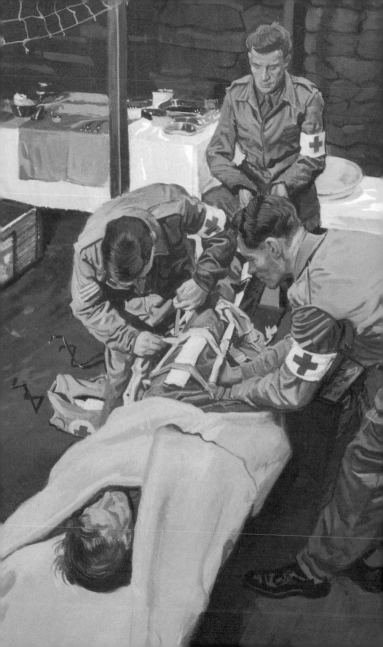

Ambulances, planes or helicopters are used to take wounded soldiers to army hospitals. The people who look after them are also in the army. Some of the nurses are men and some are women. The women belong to the Queen Alexandra's Royal Army Nursing Corps.

At times all soldiers have to see dentists. The dentists belong to the Royal Army Dental Corps. They work in rooms like your dentist.

However, some of the army dentists travel around from regiment to regiment in caravans that have been specially fitted out for them.

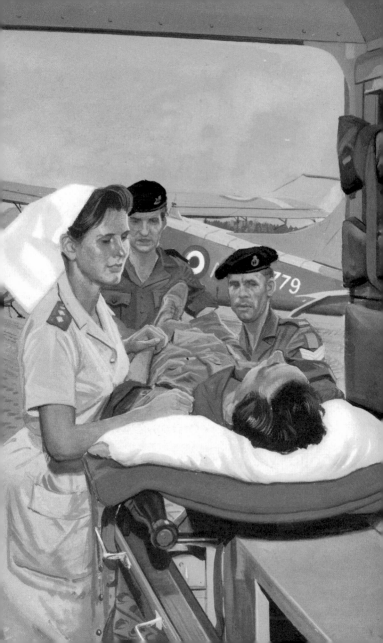

Many soldiers live together in barracks. If they have wives and children they sometimes live at home with their families. They may live in houses which belong to the army and are close to the barracks. Their children go to the nearest school just as you do.

When soldiers have free time they need not wear their uniforms. Every few months soldiers get holidays. These are called 'leave'. If the soldiers do not live near the barracks they are given tickets for free travel home on the railway.

Most of the overseas countries to which soldiers go are warmer than ours. Some of these countries are very hot and the soldiers wear special uniforms. These are made of thin cloth and sometimes have short trousers.

Soldiers in the army to-day are not treated as they were in the olden days. They are soldiers because they want to be and not because they have to be.

Soldiers are well-fed and well-clothed and are always with their friends. They have busy lives and are happy men.

Series 606B